W9-AXZ-195

INVESTIGATING
MINERALS,
ROCKS, AND
FOSSILS

INVESTIGATING MINERALS, ROCKS, AND FOSSILS

EDITED BY MICHAEL ANDERSON

Britannica
Educational Publishing

IN ASSOCIATION WITH

ROSEN
EDUCATIONAL SERVICES

Published in 2012 by Britannica Educational Publishing
(a trademark of Encyclopædia Britannica, Inc.)
in association with Rosen Educational Services, LLC
29 East 21st Street, New York, NY 10010.

First Edition

Britannica Educational Publishing
Michael I. Levy: Executive Editor, Encyclopædia Britannica
J.E. Luebering: Director, Core Reference Group, Encyclopædia Britannica
Adam Augustyn: Assistant Manager, Encyclopædia Britannica

Anthony L. Green: Editor, Compton's by Britannica
Michael Anderson: Senior Editor, Compton's by Britannica
Sherman Hollar: Associate Editor, Compton's by Britannica

Marilyn L. Barton: Senior Coordinator, Production Control
Steven Bosco: Director, Editorial Technologies
Lisa S. Braucher: Senior Producer and Data Editor
Yvette Charboneau: Senior Copy Editor
Kathy Nakamura: Manager, Media Acquisition

Rosen Educational Services
Jeanne Nagle: Senior Editor
Nelson Sá: Art Director
Cindy Reiman: Photography Manager
Matthew Cauli: Designer, Cover Design
Introduction by Jeanne Nagle

Library of Congress Cataloging-in-Publication Data

Investigating minerals, rocks, and fossils / edited by Michael Anderson. —1st ed.
    p. cm. — (Introduction to earth science)
"In association with Britannica Educational Publishing, Rosen Educational Services."
Includes bibliographical references and index.
ISBN 978-1-61530-500-1 (lib. bdg.)
1. Minerals—Juvenile literature. 2. Rocks—Juvenile literature. 3. Fossils—Juvenile literature. I.
Anderson, Michael, 1972-
QE365.2.I58 2012
552—dc22

                                                                                    2010049490

Manufactured in the United States of America

On the cover, page 3: Rocky cliff faces in Arizona's Antelope Canyon. *Shutterstock.com*

Interior background istockphoto.com/Xavier Arnau

CONTENTS

I t is tempting to think of geologists (people who study rocks and minerals) as science pirates. After all, much like the buccaneers of old, they spend a great deal of time searching for buried treasure. In the case of geology, however, there are no chests filled with money and jewels. The riches geologists uncover are made of stone. The nature and importance of these earthy treasures is the focus of this book.

As the building blocks of the Planet Earth—indeed, the very stuff of which the world is made—minerals and rocks are priceless treasures. Beyond that, their worth can be measured by their usefulness. For instance, minerals are important nutrients that every living thing on Earth must have in order to survive. They also make up the various types of rocks that are the components of natural and manmade creations—everything from hills and continents to buildings

A fossilized fish, embedded in rock. Michael Medford/National Geographic Image Collection/ Getty Images

and fine sculptures. When polished and cut, some rocks are transformed into valuable gemstones. These are often placed in settings of gold and silver, which are precious metals made from native minerals.

Even in their stony silence, rocks are able to tell an interesting story. For instance, sedimentary rocks are formed when several layers of material—sand, mud, and tiny pebbles—settle on top of one another and then are squeezed together by pressure and cemented by dissolved minerals. The layers, called strata, remain visible once the rock has been formed. Using the strata like a timeline, scientists are able to piece together the geologic history of the location where the rock was discovered.

Rocks that are formed when mineral crystals within super-hot lava, or magma, cool are called igneous rocks. The texture and amount of crystals in igneous rock provide clues about volcanic action underground and how long it took magma to cool and form structures such as mountains. Likewise, metamorphic rocks, which are formed when sedimentary or igneous rocks undergo changes to their shape or mineral structure, reveal how hot and pressurized it was deep beneath Earth's surface during certain periods of time.

Anyone wanting to know about the evolution of inorganic, or nonliving, elements of Earth should look to rocks and minerals. Fossils, on the other hand, provide a glimpse of a long-ago living world. Plant leaves, primordial sea creatures, and the feet of prehistoric mammals all have left imprints in material that has turned to stone. The cells of living trees that petrify, turning hard as a rock, and the buried skeletons of prehistoric creatures are fossils, too. By studying fossils, scientists can tell where the ancestors of today's plants and animals lived, how they survived, and when certain species became extinct.

Owning a diamond mine or holding the deed to land that has large deposits of minerals such as copper or iron could make a person rich. In general, however, smaller collections of minerals, rocks, and fossils won't make someone a millionaire. Yet the wealth of information these Earth components hold makes them true treasures indeed.

CHAPTER 1
EARTH'S BUILDING MATERIALS

E arth's building materials are minerals and rocks. Minerals are natural substances that combine to form rocks, and rocks are the basic unit that make up the

A geologist examines a sample of granite using a magnifying loupe.
InStock Photographic Ltd./Photodisc/Getty Images

solid Earth. A rock may be made up of one or more minerals. Pure sandstone, for example, consists only of the mineral quartz. Granite is composed chiefly of three minerals—quartz, feldspar, and mica. A "recipe" with different mineral ingredients results in a different kind of rock.

Scientists who study minerals and rocks work in the fields called mineralogy and petrology. Mineralogy includes the study of the physical and chemical properties of minerals, their forms, and the various ways in which they are distinguished from one another. Petrology deals with the origin, occurrence, composition, structure, and history of rocks. Because most rocks consist of minerals, the two fields are closely related. Both mineralogy and petrology fall within the broader science of geology, which is concerned with the origin of Earth, its history, its shape, the materials forming it, and the processes that are acting and have acted on it.

CHARACTERISTICS OF MINERALS

To be classified as a mineral, a substance must have an inorganic, or nonliving, origin and a composition that can be expressed by a chemical formula. Its elements may be

metallic or nonmetallic. Most minerals have a crystalline structure.

By this definition, the resin amber and the fuels coal, petroleum, and natural gas are not true minerals. These substances were formed from organic substances—animal or vegetable matter—that once lived on Earth.

The important metallic and nonmetallic mineral beds that are mined today were deposited over long periods of geologic time as a result of such natural phenomena as weathering and erosion. Other processes contributing to the concentration of minerals in the earth are sedimentation, precipitation, and evaporation of water bodies, as well as the circulation of groundwater.

Minerals are essential to the life of plants and animals. Most plants get minerals from the soil. Animals, including humans, obtain them from plants, vegetables, and fruits or from the milk, eggs, and meat of plant-eating animals.

THE ABUNDANCE OF ROCKS

Rock makes up the solid crust of Earth. Beneath the crust are pockets of molten rock, called magma. Certain hard substances formed from the remains of animals and

Black granite being mined in a Zimbabwe quarry. Desmond Kwande/ AFP/Getty Images

plants are also called rock. Coal, which is composed of plant material, is an example. Limestone contains the shells and skeletons of sea creatures and limy masses built by plants.

The soil is made up largely of rock that has been broken down by weathering. One kind of rock is eaten every day. This is salt, a rock composed of the mineral halite. Granite, limestone, sandstone, slate, and marble are rocks

known as building stones. They are removed from the earth by a process called quarrying.

Buried treasure lies in the rocks. Some of their minerals are highly valued jewels, such as diamonds, emeralds, and rubies. Gold and silver, iron, copper, and the miracle metals of the atomic age, uranium and thorium, are among the minerals essential to modern civilization. These are taken from the earth by mining.

IDENTIFYING MINERALS AND ROCKS

Scientists identify minerals by certain important properties. These include hardness, cleavage, and color. Other means of distinguishing a mineral are its elasticity and strength, specific gravity, radioactivity, and thermal, electrical, and magnetic properties. Luminescence, or the emission of light, sometimes permits rapid detection of some minerals, including some uranium ores.

The hardness of minerals is usually stated in terms of the Mohs scale. The scale ranks minerals as follows, from softest to hardest: (1) talc, (2) gypsum, (3) calcite, (4) fluorite, (5) apatite, (6) orthoclase, (7) quartz, (8) topaz,

(9) corundum, (10) diamond. The mineral with the higher number can scratch anything beneath it or equal to it in hardness. Thus a diamond can scratch everything. A mineral that will scratch apatite but not orthoclase has a rank in hardness of between 5 and 6.

Purple fluorite crystal, showing multisided planes, or cleavage. **Shutterstock.com**

Cleavage describes the way a mineral splits in planes. This property, like many others, is related to the mineral's crystal structure. Mica, for example, splits in thin sheets. Halite (salt) and galena break into cubes. Fluorite has an eight-sided cleavage, and sphalerite has a 12-sided cleavage. Some minerals break into sharp, splintery pieces called fractures.

The color of a piece of mineral is not always a dependable clue to its identity. Impurities, for example, affect color. Pure quartz is colorless, but quartz occurs in many colors. The green of malachite and the blue of azurite, however, are typical of these minerals. The streak test for color is made by rubbing the mineral on a piece of white unglazed tile.

ROCK COLLECTING

Collecting rocks and minerals is a popular and worthwhile hobby. Learning to identify the minerals and fossils in rocks may lead to a career in such rewarding sciences as chemistry, physics, geology, physical geography, or paleontology.

Amateur collectors call themselves rockhounds. With a little inexpensive equipment, such as a hammer and chisel, a notebook, a magnifying glass, and a rock hunter's guide-book, a collector is ready to gather specimens.

Rocks and minerals can be picked up almost anywhere—quarries and mines, road cuts, building excavations, beaches, stream-beds, rock outcroppings, and exposed cliffs. Most rockhounds specialize, rather than try to collect all the thousands of known miner-als. Colorful and beautifully shaped crystals are prized by all collectors. Petrified woods and fossils are interesting specialties.

Collections of semiprecious stones such as agates, zircons, garnets, and amethysts may lead to gem cutting and jewelry making. This offshoot of mineral collecting has become a major hobby in itself.

Some collectors make dramatic exhibits with fluorescent minerals. In normal light the specimens appear dull and unattractive. In a dark room, exhibited under purple light, they glow in spectacular colors. Inexpensive argon electric bulbs may be used to illuminate a box of specimens.

Many rockhounds band together in a min-eral or gem society. Local and state societies belong to one of six regional federations. These in turn are affiliated with the American Federation of Mineralogical Societies. A local or state natural-history museum can supply the address of the nearest society. These groups hold conventions at which individuals exhibit their collections, exchange specimens, and dis-cuss every aspect of their hobby.

The rough surface of the tile grinds the edge of the mineral to a powder. The color of the powder may be different from that of the solid piece. Related to the color of a mineral are its transparency and iridescence, or the play of colors in its interior or exterior.

The term luster refers to the general appearance of a mineral surface in reflected light. The main types of luster are metallic and nonmetallic. Metallic refers to the luster of an untarnished metallic surface such as gold, silver, copper, or steel. These materials are opaque; no light passes through them, even at thin edges. Nonmetallic luster is characteristic of light-colored minerals that transmit light, either through thick portions or at least through their edges. Nonmetallic minerals may appear glassy, greasy, silky, or pearly.

Every mineral has a particular specific gravity, or density. It may be determined by weighing the mineral in the air and then suspended in water. The weight in the air divided by the difference in weight when in water, is the specific gravity.

CHAPTER 2
TYPES OF MINERALS

There are several thousand known mineral species. About 100 of them, the so-called rock-forming minerals, constitute the major mineral components of rocks. Minerals can be classified into 13 groups according to their constituents. The major groups are: (1) native elements; (2) sulfides; (3) sulfosalts; (4) oxides and hydroxides; (5) halides and borates; (6) carbonates; (7) nitrates and iodates; (8) phosphates, vanadates, and arsenates; (9) sulfates; (10) tungstates and molybdates; and (11) silicates.

The names of most minerals, usually ending in the suffix -ite, are a kind of shorthand description or history of their substance. Some are named for the scientists who discovered them, others for the locations where they were first found, and still others for outstanding physical or chemical properties.

NATIVE ELEMENTS

Most minerals are composed of two or more elements, but a few consist of only

one element. The most abundant of the native metals are gold, silver, copper, and platinum. Native iron occurs in meteorites, but in the Earth it is combined with other elements.

Mercury, lead, tin, and zinc are also metals found in the native, or uncombined, form. Carbon exists in two native forms—graphite and diamond. The most common nonmetallic native element is sulfur.

SULFIDE MINERALS

The sulfides include the majority of ore minerals from which metals are obtained. Lead sulfide forms the mineral galena, silver sulfide forms argentite, and zinc sulfide forms

A nugget of gold, one of the most abundant native metals. Shutterstock.com

sphalerite. These minerals are often found together as ores.

Two important sulfides of arsenic are realgar and orpiment. Antimony sulfide is called stibnite. Antimony is alloyed, or mixed together, with lead for casting the type metal used in printing. The mineral cinnabar is a sulfide of mercury. Molybdenum, a metal that is used in alloy steels, is obtained from molybdenite, a sulfide of the metal.

The glister of pyrite has led many people to believe they had discovered nuggets of gold. **Shutterstock.com**

Three other iron sulfides, all differing slightly in chemical composition, are pyrite, marcasite, and pyrrhotite. Pyrite is known as fool's gold because its brilliant yellow

ORES

An ore is a natural combination of minerals from which metals can be extracted at a profit. Originally the term ore was applied only to metallic minerals, but the term now includes nonmetallic substances that have been deposited in rock after its formation.

All metals come from ore deposits found in Earth's crust. Raw ores bear little resemblance to familiar metals such as chromium or nickel. In most cases, the metals in the ores are not in the free, or pure, state. They are in chemical combination with other elements. They are combined with oxygen as oxides, with sulfur as sulfides, and with carbon and oxygen as carbonates. Ores also contain earthy materials such as sand and clay. These substances are separated and discarded.

Large ore deposits can mean great wealth to a country. The struggle for economic and political control of ores has gone on between nations for thousands of years. An industrial country can process its ores to produce valuable metallic products. If a country is not technically developed, it can sell its raw ores to industrialized countries.

luster somewhat resembles that of flakes of native gold.

The copper sulfides exist as minerals called chalcocite and covellite. Many ore bodies consist of sulfides containing both copper and iron. These include the minerals bornite and chalcopyrite.

The minerals classified as sulfosalts are similar to the sulfides. These are made up of sulfur, plus the metals copper, lead, or silver, combined with arsenic, antimony, or bismuth. An example is enargite, a copper arsenic sulfide.

OXIDE AND HYDROXIDE MINERALS

The oxide group includes the silicon oxide quartz, also called silica. One of the most common minerals, quartz occurs in many areas in a variety of forms. Semiprecious gem stones of quartz include amethyst, tigereye, agate, and onyx. Siliceous sinter, or geyserite, is an impure quartz deposited by hot springs and is a form of opal. The fire opal has an internal iridescence of intense orange to red.

Diatomaceous earth, or diatomite, was formed from the siliceous shells of diatoms, microscopic algae found in fresh water and

seawater. It is also called kieselguhr and tripolite. The powdery substance is used for insulating and filtering material and in the manufacture of polishing and scouring powders. Another abundant oxide of silicon is tridymite.

Among the oxides of metals that exist as minerals are cuprite, or copper oxide; zincite, or zinc oxide; cassiterite, or tin oxide;

Diatomaceous earth is formed from the powdery remains of microscopic algae shells. © www.istockphoto.com/Imageegaml

and rutile, or titanium oxide. Pyrolusite, or manganese oxide, is the chief ore of manganese. Among the ores of iron are the oxides hematite and magnetite. Lodestone, a form of magnetite, is a natural magnet. Ilmenite, which exists in large deposits, is a mixed oxide of iron and titanium. It is a chief source of the titanium used as a paint pigment and as a purifier in alloys.

Aluminum oxide, known in mineralogy as corundum (and in an impure form as bauxite), exists in two transparent and colored gem forms—sapphire and ruby. Emery, which is a black, granular rock consisting of corundum mixed with iron minerals, is used in a powdered form for grinding and polishing. Spinel is a mixed oxide of magnesium and aluminum, and chromite is an iron and chromium oxide that makes up the chief ore of chromium. Chromium is one of the major components of stainless steels.

The leading radioactive minerals, sources of such elements as radium, thorium, and uranium, include uraninite, carnotite, and autunite. They are all complex oxides of the radioactive and other elements and usually contain lead. Pitchblende, in which mineral radioactivity was first discovered, is an impure form of uraninite.

A ruby in the rough (left) and cut to create a gemstone. Rubies contain the mineral corundum, a type of aluminum oxide. **Shutterstock.com**

Hydroxides are low-temperature minerals typically formed from products of aqueous alteration or from hydrothermal vents. Among the hydroxide minerals are the aluminum ore bauxite and limonite, an iron ore containing hydrated iron oxides.

HALIDE AND BORATE MINERALS

The halides, which are soluble in water, account for relatively few minerals, but some of them have commercial value. The most outstanding of these is sodium chloride, or common salt. It is known in its mineral form as halite.

Fluorite, sold commercially as fluorspar, is composed of calcium fluoride. It is used as a flux in metallurgical processes. The rare, clear crystals of the mineral are valuable in making lenses and prisms for optical systems used with ultraviolet light. Cryolite is a fluoride of aluminum and sodium.

The borates are compounds of boron and oxygen. Most borate minerals are rare, but some form large deposits that are mined commercially. Most borate minerals occur in dried-up basins fed by waters rich in volcanic material. Borax is a borate mineral that is used in many ways — for example, as a component of glass and pottery glazes in the ceramics industry and as a fertilizer additive, a soap supplement, a disinfectant, a mouthwash, and a water softener. Other borate minerals include kernite, a hydrous (water-containing) sodium borate, and colemanite, a hydrous calcium borate.

CARBONATE MINERALS

The carbonates make up one of the largest groups of minerals. Among these is the plentiful mineral called calcite, or calcium carbonate. Large transparent crystals of calcite are called Iceland spar. This chemically pure, clear calcite—capable of producing double refraction of light—is used in prisms for polarizing microscopes and similar optical instruments.

Ordinary limestone consists largely of calcite. Marble is composed of crystalline, metamorphosed limestone. The various colors in marbles are created by chemical impurities or by veins of other minerals. The stalagmites and stalactites found in caves usually consist of calcite.

Marl is an impure limestone that is imperfectly hardened. Chalk is a soft, fine-grained limestone formed in the oceans from deposits of the shells of tiny sea animals.

Magnesite is a magnesium carbonate. It frequently occurs mixed with calcite, forming a calcium magnesium carbonate called dolomite, or dolomitic limestone. Two copper carbonates are malachite and azurite. An increase in the water content of

Slabs of marble, smoothed and ready for use. Color patterns occur due to chemical impurities and minerals that are present when limestone morphs into marble. Shutterstock.com

azurite, which is blue, can change it into malachite, which is green. Both crystals are used in jewelry.

The carbonate of iron appears as the mineral siderite. Manganese carbonate, called rhodochrosite, occurs usually as a gangue mineral with other ores.

NITRATE, IODATE, AND PHOSPHATE MINERALS

Nitrates and iodates are structurally related to carbonates. The nitrates of potassium and

Bags of ammonium nitrate being seized by Filipino police. A common ingredient in commercial fertilizers, ammonium nitrate also can be used to manufacture bombs and other explosives. **Therence Koh/AFP/ Getty Images**

of sodium exist as minerals known respectively as niter, or saltpeter, and soda niter, or Chile saltpeter. Nitrates are used in the manufacture of explosives and fertilizers. Much rarer than nitrates, iodates are yellow minerals. Among the iodates are lautarite and dietzeite.

The mineral salts of phosphoric acid that contain the element phosphorus are called phosphates. Apatite is an abundant phosphate of calcium that contains fluorine. An impure form of apatite is the phosphate rock used in fertilizers. A complicated phosphate mineral is monazite, found in beach and river sands. It is a source of the rare earth metal cerium, whose compounds are used in the glass, ceramic, photographic, and textile industries. The gem turquoise is a basic hydrous phosphate of aluminum and copper. Vanadates, compounds of vanadium and oxygen, and arsenates resemble phosphates in their crystal structure.

SULFATE MINERALS

Sulfates, which are insoluble in water and are related chemically to the saline minerals, include a barium compound called

A sample of gypsum, a sulfate mineral. Hemera/Thinkstock

barite; celestite, an ore of strontium; and alunite, a basic aluminum and potassium sulfate. Gypsum, a hydrous calcium sulfate, is the source of plaster of Paris. Transparent crystals of gypsum, known as selenite, split in thin cracks. When calcium sulfate is found uncombined with water, it is called anhydrite.

Sodium sulfate, sold commercially as Glauber's salt, exists in the hydrated form as the natural mineral mirabilite. Epsom salts—hydrous magnesium sulfate—occurs as the mineral epsomite. For commercial purposes, however, Epsom salts is manufactured from other magnesium minerals.

TUNGSTATE AND MOLYBDATE MINERALS

Salts of tung-
stic acid and
molybdic acid
are respectively
called tungstates and
molybdates. Tungsten, a
metal used in the manufacture of electric light bulbs,
steel alloys, and magnets, is
obtained chiefly from two
minerals. These are schee-
lite, or calcium tungstate,
and wolframite, which is a
mixed tungstate of the elements manganese and iron.

Nuggets of tungsten in its raw form. **Shutterstock.com**

Wulfenite is a lead molybdate. It is a minor ore of lead and molybdenum.

SILICATE MINERALS

The most widespread and numerous minerals are the silicates. They consist of silicon and oxygen combined with potassium, sodium, magnesium, aluminum, and many other elements.

Feldspars make up the most prominent group of silicates. They include orthoclase, a potassium and aluminum silicate; albite, which contains sodium instead of potassium; and oligoclase, which contains calcium in addition to sodium.

Another important silicate group includes the micas. Muscovite is the transparent mica used as an insulating material in the manufacture of electrical equipment. It consists primarily of silicate of potassium and aluminum. As isinglass it is used in devices such as stove doors and lantern shields.

A second common mica is biotite, which contains magnesium and iron; it is usually dark green, brown, or black. Another mica is lepidolite, a fluosilicate of potassium, aluminum, and lithium. Lepidolite is one of the few ores that contains the metal lithium.

A beryl emerald. Shutterstock.com

The pyroxene family contains a series of rock-forming minerals, as do the feldspar and mica groups. Two common pyroxenes are diopside, a silicate of calcium and magnesium, and augite, which contains some iron and aluminum. One variety of pyroxene is spodumene, a lithium aluminum silicate. It is sometimes found in a clear, pink crystal form called kunzite, which is used as a gem. A green variety is called hiddenite. Jadeite is another pyroxene. A true jade, it is sometimes called Chinese jade.

Other silicates form such gems as tourmaline, zircon, and topaz. Beryl, the chief ore of beryllium, is an aluminum and beryllium silicate. The emerald, whose green color is due to chromium traces, and the aquamarine are crystal forms of beryl.

A more complicated group of silicates, closely related to the pyroxenes, is the amphibole family. A variety called hornblende, containing aluminum, may occur in long, fiberlike crystals to form one kind of asbestos. Another kind of asbestos is a fibrous variety of the mineral serpentine, called chrysotile. It is the chief commercial source of asbestos. Serpentine is a hydrous magnesium silicate.

Similar to serpentine in composition is talc, the source of talcum powder. Soapstone,

A wall constructed of soapstone. iStockphoto/Thinkstock

or steatite, is an impure variety of talc. Slabs of it are used for laboratory tabletops. Talc and soapstone are ingredients of paint, ceramics, and paper.

The mineral kaolinite is a hydrous silicate, somewhat like talc, but containing aluminum instead of magnesium. The majority of clays consist of impure kaolinite, formed from the decomposition of feldspar rocks. Bentonite is a type of clay that was formed from the decomposition of volcanic ash.

Zinc silicates include willemite, which is employed in laboratory experiments because ultraviolet light renders it fluorescent. Hemimorphite, or calamine, is a hydrous zinc silicate sometimes utilized as an ore of zinc. Zeolites such as stilbite are hydrous silicates of aluminum with calcium and sodium bases. They are used as molecular sieves to separate chemicals.

CHAPTER 3
TYPES OF ROCKS

Rocks tell a fascinating story of the origin and history of Earth—a story that goes back millions of years. They tell of giant explosions and mountains that rose from the sea and then were worn down to plains, of seas that invaded the land and then retreated or dried up. They tell of blankets of ice and buried forests that turned to stone.

All rocks fall into one of three groups, according to how they were formed. These groups are igneous, sedimentary, and metamorphic rocks.

IGNEOUS ROCKS

The word igneous comes from the Latin *ignis*, meaning "fire." Igneous rocks were never actually on fire, but they were formed from very hot molten material. Igneous rocks were the first rocks.

In its beginning Earth was a mass of molten matter, or magma. It contained the elements, which are the building blocks of all matter. As the magma cooled and condensed,

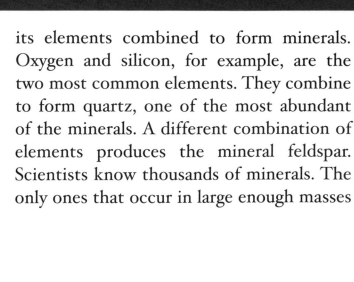

Lava flows from a volcanic eruption. Igneous rocks are formed from cooled magma (intrusive) or lava (extrusive). Greg Vaughn/The Image Bank/Getty Images

its elements combined to form minerals. Oxygen and silicon, for example, are the two most common elements. They combine to form quartz, one of the most abundant of the minerals. A different combination of elements produces the mineral feldspar. Scientists know thousands of minerals. The only ones that occur in large enough masses

to be important as rock builders, however, are quartz, feldspar, and a group called the ferromagnesian minerals. This group includes hornblende, pyroxene, biotite (black mica), olivine, and magnetite. They are dark because they contain iron and magnesium.

Igneous rocks are still being formed from pockets of magma some 40 miles (64 kilometers) underground. Magma is a hot, doughy material mixed with gases and steam. It rises along cracks in Earth's crust. If it solidifies before it reaches the surface it forms an intrusive igneous rock. If it is thrown out by volcanic action, it forms an extrusive igneous rock.

Intrusive rocks cool very slowly. Their minerals form large crystals. Granite is an example. Intrusive rocks become exposed on Earth's surface when the overlying material is worn away. Magma that erupts through volcanoes is known as lava. The material may cool so rapidly that no crystals can form. Obsidian is a glasslike rock formed in this way. The various lava rocks differ in the rapidity with which they cool and in the way their crystals form.

All lavas contain a high percentage of silica, a compound made up of the chemical

elements silicon and oxygen. Lavas containing from 65 to 75 percent silica are called rhyolites; those with 50 to 65 percent silica are andesites; and those with less than 50 percent silica are basalts.

GRANITE

The most common igneous rock in Earth's crust is granite. It commonly occurs in mountain ranges, having been formed as mountain ores. But it also occurs in level regions that were mountainous at one time but have since been worn down. Granite is made up of crystals of quartz and feldspar, usually mixed with mica and other minerals. It is one of the most frequently used building stones.

The color of granite depends on the proportions and varieties of the minerals in it. The prevailing color is gray. It is dark gray if dark minerals are abundant, and light if they are few. Greenish, pink, and blue hues are due to different kinds of feldspar. Because of its great hardness, granite is difficult to work and so is an expensive building stone.

Granite rocks along the coast of Sardinia, Italy, in the Maddalena Archipelago. **De Agostini/ Getty Images**

RHYOLITES

Rhyolites are known from all parts of the world and from all geologic ages. They melt at lower temperatures and are lighter in weight and color than basalts. Rhyolitic lavas are quite viscous, or thick, and contain large quantities of gas. The gas often boils off with explosive force, expelling large amounts of glowing ash and cinders. Sometimes,

Samples of volcanic pumice next to a seagull feather, for scale. The holes in pumice are formed when bubbles are trapped in cooling lava.
Bill Hatcher/National Geographic Image Collection/Getty Images

however, gas is released more slowly or even trapped as bubbles when the lava hardens. When the bubbles are tiny and closely packed, a lightweight stone called pumice is formed. Any kind of lava may turn into pumice, but most of it develops in rhyolites.

Pumice is used commercially for cleaning and polishing wood, metal, and other surfaces. More recently it has found use in precast masonry, poured concrete, insulation, acoustical tile, and plaster. Rhyolite pumices are white.

ANDESITES

Andesites, which are named for the Andes Mountains of South America, are a large family of rocks found in nearly all volcanic areas. Not only the Andes, where the name was first applied to a series of lavas, but most of the mountain chains of Central and North America consist largely of andesites. The same rock type occurs in abundance in volcanoes along practically the entire margin of the Pacific Basin. They are of three basic types: quartz-bearing (called dacites); hornblende- and biotite-andesites, quite rich in feldspar; and pyroxene-andesites, the most common kind.

BASALTS

Basalts are among the most abundant types of rock. They are found throughout the world. Most of the lavas that pour out of volcanoes that make up oceanic islands are basaltic. For example, the great shieldlike volcano of Mauna Loa, in Hawaii, is made up of basaltic lava flows.

Hawaii's Mauna Loa, the world's largest volcano. **Bruce Heinemann/ Stockbyte/Getty Images**

Basalts are dark gray or black in color and are denser than most other volcanic rocks. Although nearly all basaltic rock is crystalline, in some cases, where the lava has cooled rapidly, it has a glassy appearance. Because of their density and toughness, basalts are often used for making roads and in the construction of buildings.

SEDIMENTARY ROCKS

Rocks do not remain the same forever. They are broken down every day by wind, temperature changes, water, and ice. Large blocks of rock fall from cliffs. Eventually they break up into pebbles, sand, and mud. They are washed into the rivers, and the rivers spread them along their banks and deposit them at their mouths in lakes and the sea.

When these materials come to rest they are known as sediment, meaning "matter that settles." At first sediments are soft and loose. As layer settles upon layer, the overlying weight squeezes the material close together. Meanwhile dissolved mineral matter settles around the grains of the sediments and cements them together. The solid mass is then a sedimentary rock.

Sedimentary rocks can be recognized by two features. First, they are made up of materials that once were a part of older formations, such as the igneous rocks. Second, because of the sorting action of the water in which they were laid down, they lie in layers, called strata. So it is said that sedimentary rocks are stratified. Much of the North American continent is mantled with sedimentary rocks. They have been raised from the floor of the sea where they were formed on top of the older igneous rocks that mark the real crust of Earth.

SANDSTONE

Sandstone is a sedimentary rock built of grains of sand held together by a natural cement. The most common sand in sandstone is quartz, though feldspar and rock fragments

GEODES

Fossils are found in sedimentary rocks, as are geodes, which are hollow spheres that occur in limestone and sometimes shale. Geodes have an outer layer of mineral material and are usually lined with quartz crystals projecting from the inner rim toward the hollow center. They may originate as an internal cavity, such as the unfilled space within a fossil, or may expand from pressure.

The rock face of the Grand Canyon provides a spectacular example of sedimentary rock. Shutterstock.com

may also be present. The cement may consist of silica, calcium carbonate, iron oxide, lime, or clay. When quartz sand grains are tightly cemented with silica, they form the hard compact rock called quartzite.

SHALE

Shale is formed from fine-grained sediments deposited in quiet, protected waters such as the deep ocean floor, the deeper parts of continental shelves, shallow seas and bays, coastal lagoons, and river floodplains. Most shales are composed of clay minerals, quartz, and such other substances as carbonates, feldspars, iron oxides, and organic matter arranged in thin layers.

Colors in shale are caused by the presence of certain minerals and organic substances. Black shale, for example, results from organic matter, red shale from ferric iron, and green shale from ferrous iron. Shale is soft and porous, characteristics that allow it to absorb and release organic matter and minerals easily. Trapped organic material may be converted into petroleum and other hydrocarbons.

Shale has considerable economic value. It is a valuable raw material for tile, brick, and pottery and constitutes a major source

A cross-section of shale. © www.istockphoto.com/Ryan Chylinski

of alumina for portland cement. In addition, some shales yield petroleum when subjected to high heat.

LIMESTONE

Limestone is a sedimentary rock formed from the shells and skeletal remains of sea

animals such as corals. Shells and corals owe their stiffness to calcium carbonate ($CaCO_3$), often called "carbonate of lime." Limestone also is mainly calcium carbonate. Under a microscope the remains of animals that formed it can be seen.

Limestone has many important uses. It is the chief source of lime, which is used extensively as a building material and as a fertilizer. It is used in making portland cement and in smelting iron and lead, and it is an important

A limestone precipice at Denmark's Stevns Cliff. Shutterstock.com

building material. Limestone wears better than sandstone, is more easily shaped than granite, and weathers from nearly white to a beautiful gray.

CONGLOMERATES

Conglomerates and breccias are sedimentary rocks composed of coarse fragments that have been worn away from other rocks. The fragments are held together either by cement

Various rock fragments often are clearly visible in a sample of conglomerate rock. **Jeff Foott/Discovery Channel Images/Getty Images**

or by finer-grained material between them. The fragments that make up conglomerates are rounded. If the large fragments still are rough and angular, the rock is called breccia.

METAMORPHIC ROCKS

The third group of rocks is the metamorphic. The term comes from a Greek word meaning "change of form." Metamorphic rocks can be formed from both igneous and sedimentary rocks. The forces that produce them are (1) pressure and heat resulting from the shrinking and folding of Earth's crust; (2) water action, which dissolves and redeposits minerals; and (3) the action of hot magma on old rocks.

The most common metamorphic rock is gneiss (pronounced "nice"). It was originally granite. Shrinking and pressure rearranged the minerals in distinct layers. Schist and slate are metamorphosed shale. Pressure changed bituminous (soft) coal into anthracite (hard coal).

Some marble was formed by the folding and pressure on limestone. Other marble was made when water seeped through deeply buried limestone. The water dissolved the limy mineral (calcite) and rearranged the particles in little crystalline blocks. Water also changed many sandstones by depositing quartz around the grains of sand. In time each grain became a crystal, locked to other crystals. Thus the sandstone became quartzite.

Igneous, or contact, metamorphism occurred when magma was forced into older rocks. The magma squeezed the old rocks, heated them, and sent out steam that dissolved some minerals and deposited others.

A sample of banded gneiss from the Verzasca River in Switzerland. Gneiss is easily identifiable by it many colorful bands. **Andreas Strauss/LOOK/Getty Images**

In this way shale was turned into hornfels, a dark rock that resembles flint or fine-grained basalt.

Gneiss

Gneiss is medium- to coarse-grained and may contain abundant quartz and feldspar. It has a distinct banding pattern. The banding is usually due to the presence of differing proportions of minerals in the various bands; dark and light bands may alternate because of the separation of dark and light minerals. Banding can also be caused by differing grain sizes of the same minerals.

The characteristics of a particular gneiss are a result of the complex interaction of original rock composition, pressure and temperature of metamorphism, and the addition or loss of component minerals.

Schist

Schists are the second most common metamorphic rocks. They were apparently

A very common form of metamorphic rock, schist is formed in several layers that can be easily split. Shutterstock.com

formed by the partial recrystallization of shales under the action of heat and pressure. A major type is mica schist. It is composed essentially of quartz, combined usually with muscovite or biotite mica. Talc schist contains abundant talc; it has a greasy feel and a grayish-green color.

The term schist comes from a Greek word meaning "to divide" because the layers can be split apart. As the layers become narrower, the rock grades into phyllite and then into slate.

SLATE

Like shales, most slates were originally clay sediments deposited by water. These clay beds, lying far beneath Earth's surface, were subjected to relatively low temperature and pressure. As a result, slates were formed chiefly among older rocks. If the clay is deposited in layers and has a tendency to split along the bedding planes, it is shale. If it is tilted up at a new angle and was compressed so that it spread out and produced cleavage planes at right angles to the direction of pressure, it is slate. The principal minerals in slate are mica, chlorite, and quartz.

Slate comes in several shades, which can make rooftops and other structures quite colorful. **Shutterstock.com**

Slate may be black, blue, purple, red, green, or gray. It splits readily into thin slabs that have great strength and durability. It may be marketed as dimension slate or as crushed slate. Dimension slate is used mainly for electrical panels, laboratory tabletops, roofing and flooring, and blackboards. Crushed slate is used in roofing and as a filler.

The marble staircase and floors of the state capitol building in Frankfort, Ky. Architects and designers favor marble as a building material for its elegance and weatherproof and fireproof characteristics. **Michael Townsend/Photographer's Choice/Getty Images**

MARBLE

Marble was formed from limestone, which is composed of calcium carbonate, or dolomite, composed of calcium magnesium carbonate. Pure marble is white. Marble varies widely in color, however, from white to black through almost every shade of the spectrum. Impurities such as silica, iron oxides, and graphite give marble its color and characteristic rich veining and clouding. In texture it has a wide range from fine to coarse, and it takes a good polish.

Marble is easily carved for statues. Impervious to moisture and fire resistant, it is ideal for monuments and fireproof buildings. Architects use it for columns, walls, floors, and steps, both interior and exterior. Interior designers also use it to decorate such items as tabletops and fireplaces.

CHAPTER 4
FOSSILS

I f rocks tell of Earth's history, those that hold fossils contribute an especially intriguing part of the story. Fossils are remains of ancient plants and animals. In many parts of the world, if one digs long enough and deep enough, one may come across a fossil—for example, an ancient clamshell, a fragment of a big bone, a piece of petrified wood, or a leaf print. The term comes from a Latin word meaning "to dig," for fossils are usually found by digging. They may be uncovered in the excavations for the foundation of a building, in stone quarries and coal mines, and in road cuts.

The science of fossils is called paleontology, from Greek words meaning the science (*logia*) of very old (*palaios*) existing things (*onta*). The science of extinct animals is paleozoology. The science of extinct plants is paleobotany. The science that tries to establish the climate of the past from the fossils of a given locality is paleoclimatology. The science that tries to trace ancient geographical features is paleogeography.

KINDS OF FOSSILS

There are many different kinds of fossils, because countless animals and plants lived in the past and they were preserved in many different ways. Sometimes the actual bone or tooth of an extinct animal was preserved in hot, dry locations. In moist places the original bone material was replaced, cell by cell, with minerals. It thus became fossilized, or petrified. If the once-living thing was a tree, the fossil may be a part of the tree trunk, which underwent replacement of woody material with minerals.

The fossil may be what is called a stone core. The shell of an ancient snail, for example, filled with fine sand after the animal died. Eventually the shell itself disintegrated, but meanwhile the sand that filled it had turned to stone. The stone exactly reproduced the inner shape of the shell. Sometimes the body of an animal was buried. It decayed and left a hollow mold that filled up with mineral matter, forming a cast of the animal's shape.

The fossil may be simply a print. The footprint of a prehistoric animal may have been preserved under layers of sand or silt. Prints are known of fishes, of butterflylike insects,

The fossilized skull of an animal, discovered in South Africa. Over time, bone material is replaced by minerals, which is how skeletons and skulls become fossils. **Gerald Hinde/Gallo Images/Getty Images**

and even of jellyfish. The delicate imprint of a leaf or blossom on some soft material may have later hardened into solid rock. Many different kinds of plants left leaf prints.

Another kind of fossil is called an inclusion. The object is usually small—an insect or a small piece of a plant, such as a blossom. It became embedded in the flowing resin of a pinelike tree. The resin fossilized into amber, and the embedded insect became a fossil too.

Animals that became trapped in tar pits are a variety of inclusion fossils. Rancho La Brea, in Los Angeles, Calif., is the most spectacular fossil area in the United States. Its sticky pools of oil and asphalt trapped thousands of prehistoric animals, much as flypaper catches flies. Saber-toothed tigers, giant wolves, sloths, mastodons, short-faced bears, and horses have been uncovered here. The flesh decayed and became part of the tar, but the bones and teeth were well preserved.

Finally, there are pseudofossils, or false fossils. These are mineral forms that look like fossils. If two pieces of slate do not quite touch for some reason and mineral-bearing water enters the crack, the minerals may be deposited to look like fossil moss or fossil ferns. Such pseudofossils are called dendrites, from the Greek *dendron*, meaning "tree."

PETRIFIED FOREST

Over large areas of the western United States are forests that have turned to stone. More accurately, over the course of millions of years the trees' natural wood fibers have been replaced bit by bit with minerals, usually silica (silicon dioxide), and the trees are said to be silicified or petrified.

In the petrified forests of the western United States, many of the tree tissues have been replaced by chalcedony, a translucent quartz that is usually waxy pale blue or gray in color. This replacement is often so accurate that both the internal and external structure of the tree is faithfully represented, and what remains is a mineral replica of the original tree. Sometimes even the tree's cell structure is discernible in the petrified remains.

Some of the most spectacular displays of petrified wood are in the Petrified Forest National Park in eastern Arizona. About 160 million years ago this region was a lowland floodplain. Pine forests, of a species now extinct, grew about 100 miles (160 kilometers) to the southwest. The trees died of natural causes, and some of them fell into streams and floated or were washed by floods to their present location. They were rapidly covered with mud and sand, which prevented their decay. These sediments contained a large amount of volcanic ash, rich in silica. Groundwater

dissolved the silica and other minerals and deposited them in the cell tissue of the logs. This process continued very gradually until the logs were composed almost entirely of minerals. Cavities in the logs were often lined with quartz crystals. The brilliant reds and greens evident today are caused chiefly by traces of iron oxides.

Over the years the mud and sand sediments turned to sandstones and shales. These in turn were buried deep beneath fresh layers of sand and silt. When the Rocky and Sierra Nevada mountains were formed, the ancient logs were cracked. Erosion eventually removed the softer rocks and partially uncovered the petrified forests, which now lie in colorful fragments on the park's floor.

HOW FOSSILS ORIGINATED

The record of life on Earth goes back more than a billion years. The early part of the record is extremely scanty and difficult to read. Over the past 500 million years, however, starting in the Cambrian era of Earth's history, many plant and animal remains have been preserved. From these remains the evolutionary history of life has been worked out. It is amazing that so much has been discovered, when one considers how very remote are the possibilities that even fossilized

A Japanese museum displays the head and tusks of a prehistoric mammoth that had been found frozen in a Siberian permafrost zone. Koichi Kamoshida/Getty Images

material could survive through such enormous periods of time.

Most animal fossils are those of creatures that died an accidental death in such a way that their bodies were quickly covered over. An animal that drowned near a river mouth and was swept out to sea and covered with sand and silt may have become fossilized. An animal that fell into a swamp or one that was covered by wind-blown sand during a storm in a desert and remained covered may be fossilized.

A special situation of fossilization occurred with the Siberian mammoths. These hairy elephants of the Pleistocene period occasionally fell into a crevasse of a glacier. Their bodies did not decay but were well preserved in the ice. These bodies remained in a subfossil state, meaning that they did not undergo the changes to make them fossils. It is known that wolves and huskies ate the flesh of such mammoths after they had thawed out.

HOW FOSSILS ARE HANDLED

Fossil hunters should have some knowledge of geology in order to recognize the kinds of places in which fossils are likely to

be found. Undisturbed sedimentary deposits are among the best possibilities. These are exposed in coal mines, road cuts, and sandstone and limestone quarries. A marble quarry would be worthless because marble is a metamorphic rock formed under conditions that would destroy any fossils in the original rock.

Once a fossil has been discovered, the first task is to remove it from the site. No attempt is made at the site to remove the fossil from the matrix, as the stone in which it is embedded is called. Instead, a piece of rock large enough to be sure that it contains the whole fossil is chiseled out. Fossils found in the mud of a river bed or in loose sand may be washed on the spot.

If the fossil site is large, it may have to be cut up with a stone saw. This requires professional skills. In addition, permission must be obtained from the owner of the site. Professionals photograph the whole site before starting to work. The pieces are numbered as they are cut out, so that they can be put together exactly as they were found.

Sometimes a fossil that has weathered out of the rock has become soft and crumbly in the weathering process. In that case a different procedure is followed. Burlap is

A geologic conservator prepares a dinosaur skeleton for display at a museum in Bristol, England. Handling fossils and fossilized remains requires precision and a delicate touch. **Matt Cardy/Getty Images**

soaked with wet plaster of Paris and wrapped around the exposed end of the bone. Then the block of stone is cut out, and the whole is wrapped in more burlap soaked in plaster of Paris before it is crated for shipment. If the fossil is something that might be damaged if it is moved, such as a footprint or a leaf print, plaster casts are made on the spot.

The most difficult process is freeing the fossil from the matrix. The instruments used are the sculptor's chisel for the rough work and engraving tools and dental drills for the fine work. Those who undertake this work must know the particular kind of extinct animal on which they are working. They must know where every bone is supposed to be. They must also be able to guess where the bones might be if the fossil has been squeezed out of shape by the weight of the rock.

After the fossils have been freed from their matrix they must be carefully preserved. Glue is applied to the cracks, and the surface then is covered with shellac or with hot paraffin.

WHAT FOSSILS TEACH

By studying fossils, scientists have been able to piece together some of the important pages in the history of Earth and its people. They have proved that the Rocky Mountains, the Alps, and the Himalayas were once below the level of the ocean, for the remains of sea animals have been found high up on their slopes. From fossils scientists have learned also that the ancestors of the camel once roamed the plains of North America, that tropical forests once covered the United States and Europe, and that many plants once grew in the polar regions.

Fossils show that the great coal and chalk beds of the world were formed from the remains of living things. Millions of years ago tiny animals were making shells that became the limestone of today.

Fitting together the scattered parts of the fossil story, science has traced animal life back to the earliest worms and shellfish. It has shown how, one after another, there appeared cartilaginous fishes, amphibians (half-land, half-water animals such as the frog), insects, reptiles, birds and bony fishes, and mammals.

Strangest of all creatures are the giant monsters of the Era of Reptiles—the dinosaurs, the ichthyosaurs, and other scaled, horny creatures of dragonlike appearance. Some of these old reptiles were about 100

Crinoid fossils. The discovery of stony remains of crinoids and other tiny sea creatures on mountain slopes suggests that the Alps and other ranges may once have been below the ocean's surface. Mark Gibson— Rainbow/Science Faction/Getty Images

feet (30 meters) long—the largest land animals that ever lived. Those who study fossils learn from these remains that the farther back in time an animal lived, the smaller is the proportion of brain space in its skull. Hundreds of species of great size and strength died out and made way for creatures with more brain and less bulk. The latest of all fossil remains are those of early humans found mostly in the Great Rift Valley of East Africa.

CONCLUSION

The science of geology is broad, encompassing the history of Earth (including the history of life on the planet) and all physical processes at work on Earth's surface and in its crust. At its foundation, however, is the study of the planet's fundamental materials—minerals and rocks. The study of fossils also provides invaluable knowledge about prehistoric life and about Earth itself.

To understand minerals, rocks, and fossils, geologists use knowledge gained in other fields of science such as physics, chemistry, and biology. This approach allows them to better understand the workings of Earth processes through time.

The importance of minerals, rocks, and fossils cannot be overemphasized. Without fossils, people would have a much poorer understanding of what occurred in the distant past—when the Earth was formed. Without minerals and rocks, the physical world would simply not exist.

alloy A substance composed of two or more metals, or a metal and a nonmetal, that have been fused together, dissolving in each other when heated.

andesite Any of a large group of gray to black volcanic rocks containing 50 to 65 percent silica.

basalt Dark gray to black, dense to fine-grained igneous rock that consists of basic plagioclase, augite, and usually magnetite.

borate A compound of boron and oxygen.

cleavage In geology, a term that describes the type of form, with flat and straight-line surfaces, a mineral takes when it is split; for example, cubes, thin sheets, or splinters.

crystalline Made up of crystals, which are solid pieces in which the atoms are arranged in a definite pattern.

erosion When earth is worn away by water, wind, or other natural forces.

halide The combination of a halogen and another element.

igneous Crystalline or glassy noncrystalline rocks formed when magma cools and becomes solid.

insoluble Incapable of being dissolved.

iridescence When a gem or stone reflects light in such a way that a rainbow effect of colors occurs.

luminescence The property of certain minerals and other materials to send out light when they are relatively cool.

luster The appearance of a mineral's surface as it reflects light.

magma Molten, or liquefied, rock beneath Earth's surface; when cooled, it forms igneous rock.

metamorphic A type of rock that results when preexisting rocks go through changes in response to various geological conditions, including variations in temperature, pressure, and stress.

mineralogy The field of science that deals with minerals, including their physical properties, chemical makeup, and distribution in nature.

molybdate A salt made up of molybdic acid.

opaque Blocking light.

petrified When minerals and water replace living tissue, turning living matter to stone.

petrology The science that deals with the origin, history, occurrence, structure, chemical composition, and classification of rocks.

phosphates Mineral salts of phosphoric acid that contain the element phosphorus.

rhyolite Very acidic volcanic rock that contains 65 to 75 percent silica; the lava form of granite.

sedimentary A type of rock formed by or from deposits of sediment, such as sand and mud.

silicate Any of many minerals that contain silicon and oxygen in combination with other elements.

sulfide A mineral containing sulfur combined with one or more metals.

American Geological Institute
4220 King Street
Alexandria, VA 22302-1502
(703) 379-2480
Web site: http://www.agiweb.org
The American Geological Institute is a
federation of several geoscientific and
professional associations that provides
information services to Earth scientists,
strengthens geoscience education, and
increases public awareness of the vital
role the geosciences play in society.

Geological Association of Canada
Department of Earth Sciences
Room ER4063, Alexander Murray Building
Memorial University of Newfoundland
St. John's, NL A1B 3X5
Canada
(709) 864-7660
Web site: http://gac.ca
The Geological Association of Canada is a
professional organization that publishes
journals and books, bestows grants and
awards, and encourages lifelong learning
in the geological sciences.

The Geological Society of America
3300 Penrose Place

Boulder, CO 80301-1806
(303) 357-1000
Web site: http://www.geosociety.org/
The Geological Society of America provides
information and resources that enable
Earth scientists at all levels of expertise
to study the building blocks of the planet
Earth and share their scientific findings.

Geological Survey of Canada
580 Booth Street
Ottawa, ON K1A 0E4
Canada
(613) 995-0947
Web site: http://gsc.nrcan.gc.ca/index_e.php
As the premier agency for geoscience infor-
mation within the Natural Resources
Canada, the Geological Survey of
Canada offers maps, information,
technology, standards and expertise con-
cerning the Canadian landmass.

Mineralogical Society of America
3635 Concorde Parkway, Suite 500
Chantilly, VA 20151-1110
(703) 652-9950
Web site: http://www.minsocam.org
The Mineralogical Society of America
seeks the advancement of mineralogy,

crystallography, geochemistry, and petrology in other sciences, industries, and the arts. Generating publications, educational courses and lectures, meetings, and grants helps the organization meet its goals.

Paleontological Society
Department of Geology and Environmental
    Sciences
P.O. Box 9044
Boulder, CO 80301
(330) 972-7633
Web site: http://paleosoc.org
The Paleontological Society disseminates information and current research on fossils to paleontologists—new and experienced, professional and amateur—through publications and meetings.

Society for Sedimentary Geology
4111 S Darlington, Suite 100
Tulsa, OK 74135-6373
(800) 865-9765
Web site: http://www.sepm.org
The not-for-profit Society for Sedimentary Geology provides information on sedimentology, stratigraphy, paleontology, environmental sciences, and other related geologic specialties. The society

publishes scientific journals, offers courses, and hosts conferences and other meetings.

WEB SITES

Due to the changing nature of Internet links, Rosen Educational Services has developed an online list of Web sites related to the subject of this book. This site is updated regularly. Please use this link to access the list:

http://www.rosenlinks.com/ies/rock

BIBLIOGRAPHY

Casper, Julie Kerr. *Minerals: Gifts from the Earth* (Chelsea House, 2007).

Garcia, F.A., and D.S. Miller *Discovering Fossils: How to Find and Identify Remains of the Prehistoric Past* (Stackpole, 1998).

Hall, Cally. *Gemstones* (DK, 2010).

Mitchell, J.R. *The Rockhound's Handbook* (Gem Guides, 2008).

Parker, Steve. *The World Encyclopedia of Fossils and Fossil-Collecting* (Lorenz, 2007).

Polk, Patti. *Collecting Rocks, Gems, and Minerals* (Krause, 2010).

Pough, F.H. *Peterson First Guide to Rocks and Minerals* (Houghton, 1991).

Russell, Henry. *Encyclopedia of Rocks, Minerals, and Gemstones* (Thunder Bay, 2001).

Symes, R.F. et al. *Rocks and Minerals* (DK, 2008).

Thompson, Ida. *National Audubon Society Field Guide to North American Fossils* (Knopf, 2007).